Jude Aquilina grew up in suburban Magill and now lives in Milang beside Lake Alexandrina. Her poetry, stories and articles have been published in newspapers and literary journals across Australia and abroad. Jude has taught creative writing at Flinders University, TAFESA and in high schools, community centres, libraries and a prison. In 2018, she was awarded the Barbara Hanrahan Fellowship. She is a freelance writer, editor, teacher and mentor who enjoys helping people on their writing journeys. Jude lives at Milang on the shores of Lake Alexandrina, where she enjoys gardening, rural life, and collecting old bits and bobs.

Franz Kempf A.M. is a painter and print-maker, represented by works in National, State and Regional Collections in Australia, the USA, England, Israel and China. In 2003 he was awarded the Order of Australia for his contribution to the Arts. His books published by Wakefield Press include *Franz Kempf – Thinking on Paper* (2003), *Days of Masks and Riddles* (2010), and *Franz Kempf: Aspects of a Journey 1947–2016* (2016). Franz Kempf died in February, 2020.

Other works by Jude Aquilina

Knifing the Ice
Wakefield Press, 2000

Co-editor of *Friendly Street 24*
Wakefield Press, 2000

Woman Speak (with Louise Nicholas)
Wakefield Press, 2009

Thread me a Button (with Joan Fenney)
Ginninderra Press, 2012

Ship Tree
Picaro Press, 2012

Editor of *Tadpoles in the Torrens: Poems for young readers*
Wakefield Press, 2013

Beauty and the Breast
Garron Publishing, 2013

Furry Tales
Ginninderra Press, 2015

Editor of *Milang Station*
Encompass Designs, 2018

On a moon spiced night

Jude Aquilina

Illustrations by Franz Kempf

Wakefield Press

Wakefield Press
16 Rose Street
Mile End
South Australia 5031
www.wakefieldpress.com.au

First published 2004
Reprinted 2006
This edition published 2022

Cover etching by Franz Kempf
Designed and typeset by Ryan Paine

ISBN 978 1 86254 640 0

A catalogue record for this book is available from the National Library of Australia

Wakefield Press thanks Coriole Vineyards for continued support

For my mother and friend, Joan

Contents

Habitat

Love's dream

Seeds

Creature acts

Habitat

Sultry

The street breathes into my sleep-out
huffs heat through fly screens.
The pale starless sky
is a backdrop for barking dogs.
An orange street light
inflames a row of garbage bins.

A V-8 engine throbs along the highway
and I imagine an orange Monaro
clinging like a fly to a strip of tar
trying to escape.

Yesterday, by the petrol station
I saw a bronze girl hitchhiking
dusty as an unearthed statue
poised arm, tapered thumb
and singlet arm-holes stretched
enough to see a dangerous curve.

Embalmed in sheets and sweat
I drift and toss and dream
of her long plaited hair
burning in the sunset.
Air-brakes squeal,
a round of dogs fires up.
I hitch myself to daybreak.

Bussing it

First hours, you're alert, red dirt dreaming, gleaning movement from flatness: wedge-tailed eagles rise from road-kill; a russet dingo glances over a bony shoulder before seeping back into sand. Later, no best-seller can hold you. You're part of this amorphous, wriggling, grunting mass which winds through night on a grey snail trail. The sun comes up, passes over, goes down. Telegraph wires are staves for a melody of stars played on the veins of sleepless eyes. Gears change up. Gears change down. We stop at every tin-shed shop, every rusty mailbox, until I wonder how many stops are contrived because the driver is a smoker. Six am, I'm certain he's a sadist when he plays *Teenage Ninjas* on video, full volume, not a kid on board. The young woman next to me smiles, explains, *That's why we nurses rattle trolleys, raise voices, to check for morning movements, vital signs.* Maybe this is what it's like on your final journey: numb, immobilised, cruising through space to an unknown place. Please god, on the bus to heaven with my number on it, let there be a non-smoking driver, a young nurse beside me, and just a little more leg room.

Poem after 500 km

My body buried
deep in the lamb's-wool seat
of a Ford Falcon wagon
I am merely eyes and vibrations.
Telegraph poles flash by
black crosses against dusk.
Dry grass blurs a golden frame
around a mythical three legged horse.

My eyes swim in surreal time,
a dish of late sunlight shimmers.
White lines turn silver,
engine silent, I could be gliding
on a current to heaven.

A truck's air-horn
trumpets me back to bitumen
like an angel.

CITY

Window
sequined
towers rise:
child's play
trying hard
to reach
the sky.
Clusters
of angular
fungi
clone
in fertile
smog.

Old facades
in cement
boots
squeezed
by progress,
seized by
choking
tar-vines.

Two clocks
preside,
call order
on the hour,
deafen
pedestrians
like judges
vying for
conviction
on upturned
faces.

Nightly
the pin-wheel
blurs as
traffic hurls
fumes
past cafe
crowds that
spew
onto streets
music slinks
from taxis
spittle and
piss dance on
the curb the
beast breathes
and glows.

In alcoves
between tall
walls, the
remains of a
campsite: a
singed pillow
quilt of news
mattress of
grass & glass.
Still life with
flagon & shoe.

In the Queen's Arms

Every town's front bar has its
Sid James, Yootha Joyce, a Jesus lookalike
and a couple of Buddhas.
From the white hats of bowlers
to blue singlets and bikie jackets
characters recycle each generation
knocking back a nip, a pony or a pint
of whatever the era ferments.

Music swirls from a jukebox
local fiddlers, pipers
get stompers and songsters going.
Story tellers cite comic tragedies
self-heroes battle and disappear.
Each Friday night in that bitter happy hour
punters float in a stream of ale,
clear spirits, betting slips.

Sometimes, a violin and tin whistle
transform stone walls
into mirrors of past:
beaten copper plaques
of semi-stoic men with mugs
a laughing skirt at their side
Jesus, Yootha, Sid and Buddhas
all smiling from behind.

Gulp

I do not want to be swallowed
by this multi-storey, moving stairway
express line, cash register city
this triple-lane, 60k, traffic jam
one-way, honk for your team city
this join the queue, no standing,
butts here, no exchange, come again city
this open 24 hours, no refund
mind your step, fully disposable city

I do not want to be swallowed
by this jack-hammer, spent condom,
hard hat, potted tree, this way please city
this in-only, self cleansing, sanitised,
homogenised, thanks for visiting city
this genetically modified, hypo-allergenic
sealed for your protection, pre-paid city
this crinkle free, high UV, adults only
red light, all night, triple X city.
I do not want to be swall . . . oh . . .

NYE Generic

New Years Eve, that nanosecond non-event.
An esky full of hopes hinged on midnight.
The marquee, a white hive buzzing. I'm part
of the swarm, the work-force sent to flutter
around the light, to relive the ritual
and possibly procreate. The climax comes,
as it always does, someone yells *shut-up*
and revs up the radio. In ten short seconds the year
flashes by. I try to remember a resolution. I should . . .

I should . . . Who cares? It's just another 365 days
of sinking or swimming, of making noise
or being silent, of steamy love or cleaning floors.

Dodging bear hugs and beery moustaches,
I kiss more people than I have all year.
The party's faces; amber honeycomb of bottles
all captured inside this canvas hive. The band
beats on for the lovers whose tongues kiss in corners,
for singles circling closer, for children asleep under trestles.
A last hiss of keg, and a few merry lads help the band
sing *Khe Sanh*. And so begins another year,
half here, half there, scribbling lines in the air.

Grace versus The Highway

Wearing her face like a domett shroud
Grace weaves between days of domestic decay
and nights with Chopin and Strauss.
Inside her ramshackle temple
the bible radio babbles, weevils breed
and last week's apple-crumble grows fur.

She watches the buses through parted lace.
After seventy years of service, the tea trolley
creaks no more and the lead crystal is grey.
Her sons are old men in foreign cities
her pets have fertilised the rampant ivy
and the busy street is stranger than tv.

A hanging garden chokes verandah posts;
violets and agapanthus bury the pathways.
Entwined in her nest, Grace is safe for now
until the rats in suits and ties arrive
bearing smiles and papers to sign.
Her shrine will be desecrated by July.

Street Fabric

Chiffon
cooks sponge cakes
decorates with silver roses
and sugared butterflies.

Fleecy
red cheeks, pony tail
jogs through winter leaves
whistling to her shaggy dog.

Nylon
stands at the gate
in fluffy orange slippers
chats in hot rollers.

Calico
clear skinned, earthy
sits by potted ferns
weaving cane swans.

Crepe
a cameo on her lapel
velvet hair and high heels
catches taxis to David Jones.

Hand knit
keeps safety-pins
in the brim of her felted hat
gives zucchinis to neighbours.

Crimplene
is crinkled and stooped
light blue slacks in the garden
pearls and gloves on Sunday.

Leather
skols iced-coffee
outside the local deli
belches as she revs her Ducati.

Adelaide, 1970s

I'm watching a man in a grey dust-coat weigh my mother on the great red scales. The needle spins a sigh. Then we mount the speckled marble stairs to Coles Cafeteria, past ladies on public phones, parcels piled at their feet, to a massive room of many voices, chook-house-loud, muffled, shrill. Cups and plates rattle-clanging on stainless steel trays. Chrome chairs scraping. Espresso machines hiss-steam at a team of hair-netted staff, whose hands are never still. We order pasties, chips and jelly cups.

We 'spend a penny' at John Martin's Ladies' Lounge, then sit plush in a dress circle of lighted mirrors, the air thick with powder and hair-spray. I stare into a matrix of mirrored women. If I'm good – really good – and don't tug at my mother's handbag at Moore's closing-down sale where crowds of women fossick amongst the marble pillars for stockings and scarf-rings; if I walk all the way to Miller Anderson's, the one-stop-shop for sensibly shod matrons and blue rinse grannies, then maybe we'll catch that rattly old elevator to heaven, to Cox Foys' roof-top Ferris wheel which ferries families over the edge and back again.

In Rundle Street – cars fume, buses belch. My hand squeezed tight we cross mid-stream to buy minimum chips: 15 cents, wrapped in newspaper, an air vent torn in one corner. Groceries in brown paper bags. An STA ticket-seller works the line with his low-slung leather pouch and worn coin sorter. Our bus tickets have messages of wisdom, like: *Faith will never die as long as coloured seed catalogues are printed.*

Down Hindley Street, sleazy young men in nylon body-shirts cruise in brown Fords and Sandman panel vans, repeating the same songs on their rock-boxes as they loop and leer. There are business men in safari suits, wide ties and long socks, joggers in tight bright satin shorts, and platformed women hurrying past in huge sun-glasses and boob tubes, careful not to puncture the air with a nipple.

I see Nellie the mechanical elephant smoking at John Martin's Christmas pageant; Pop-eye putt-putting along the Torrens, beside the stick-insect rowers. Upstream, Samorn the zoo elephant dances her rhythms of boredom or takes kids for rides, round and round for a peanut on a post. Naughty boys give her peppered bread. George the orang-outang, sitting with his thoughts.

The Postie on a pushbike blows a whistle to warn masses of frenzied dogs. The Tip Top Baker delivers bread in baskets from a slow red van. Bottle-Oh calls once a month, tinkles down the driveway, a sackful of brown glass on his back. The milkman rises early to foil the sun and milk-money-thieves. Old men ride push bikes with cartons or kit bags strapped to their carriers. House doors are left unlocked. Asleep on the lawn on summer nights.

A blink and it all turns black and white.

Pointillism

Sitting amongst   myselves
leafless limbs of   a winter walnut tree
mossy branches   branching mossy
I feel the wet paint   cool on my skin. I am
a Russian doll   an infinity of sisters
layers peeled, gained   a million dots
on a closed circuit tv   screening this moment
a documentary –   never to be shown again.

Tunnel Vision

Inside
my kaleidoscope people
rotate in luminous green and
neon purple against an
orange fuzz of cars and
honeycomb houses. Suns and
moons appear, blue years
disappear until my eyes
stream, trapped in a tunnel of
fading light; moments lost in
cloud like the sequins in a
lake's veil. Often, I am one
vicious shake away from
madness. I want to swim into
the black, break walls, spill
the truth that what we see is
so much less than
what could be.

In Search of Nothing in Six Easy Steps

1. Mirror yourself and your actions.
   Choose to move or be still.

2. Measure length and breadth of a cloud.
   Change depends, depend on change.

3. Switch TV channels every 7 seconds.
   See reflections of your own chaos.

4. Follow a ball which you kick aimlessly.
   The lost sometimes find new paths.

5. Photograph 100 people without film.
   Memories print more than ink.

6. Knit an invisible scarf. Wear this scarf.
   Remember each dropped stitch.

When you find nothing, celebrate
and hold it in your heart forever.

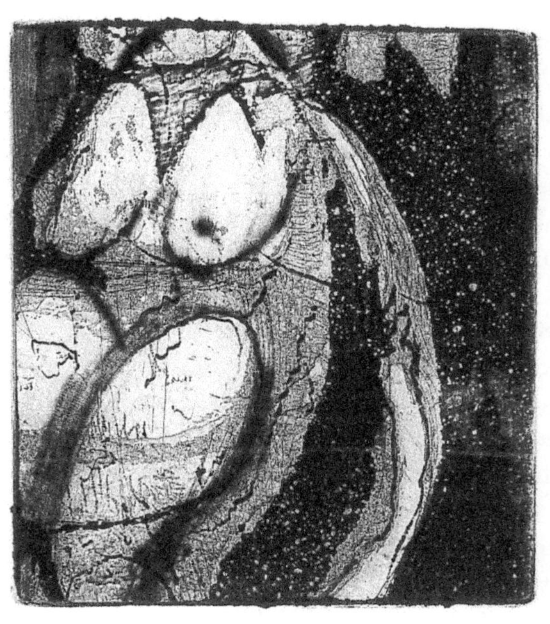

Love’s dream

On the road to love

40 km/h

Willy, a blonde Kombi van,
purred his words slowly as he drove.
Often wedged to the axles in sand,
he took extended holidays waiting
in sunny deserts for engine parts to come.
His turtle shell impenetrable – I never did get to drive.

60 km/h

Cedric was a pale green Toyota Crown
with self-installed fan, a horn, thick and atonal.
His picnic hamper and multi-coloured tin cups,
a symbol of his reliability.

100 km/h

Dave was a Monaro
a he-man 70s type, heavy and thirsty
tromping his foot on the bar stool rung
singing along to Led Zeppelin.
His orange duco reddened when you turned him on.

160 km/h

And Pino was a Lamborghini
with fluffy dice and horn of fertility.
Once we careered around curves and hair-pin bends
into the leafy fringes of forest.
But next time, he drove straight past me
to pick up my girlfriends, one by one.

The Lonesome Cowgirl Blues

Hey there, hip-wigglin cowboy, I wanna take you
home, plug you into my amp, I'll fiddle while you
croon sweet tunes about how long since you've been
kissed, we'll sing the wrinkles out of those satin dacks.

Don't take your spurs off honey, I wanna see sparks
on the mirrored ceiling as your saddle sways, bucks
to the beat. I wanna feel like Dolly P when I hold
your hard mike between my parted pouted lips.

I'll howl like a prairie dog under full moon
slide my fingers along your hot fret board
lasso your tongue – just let me hear you strum
The Lonesome Cowgirl Blues, one more time.

Diary of a Poisoner

Just a drop of clear liquid, a pinch of powder
no violence, no hate-bulging eyes just a slow
mellow phase, a winding down as I hold your hand.
We visit health-shops and puzzled doctors.
I stroke your hair, lead you like a tired child
to your chamber.

I love you all the more when you are grasping
for me. My sympathy is my gift I believe it myself
you really *do* have a weak heart aren't you lucky
to have me as I innocently serve your favourite
mushroom soup with a dollop of cream.

You've given up the grog, a grey complexion suits you
far better than sherry red. Your friends at the pub
have forgotten you, it's less stress.
I actually left the Poisonous Plants book on the coffee table
you began reading called to me *Did you know*
that many boys die instantly from fashioning whistles
from the stalks of Hemlock?

A tune as fatal as a Siren's, I replied humming.
We both laughed until you coughed and I pushed a pillow
into the small of your back, wiped the tea leaves
from your chin, massaged the nape of your neck.

Animi Causa

Blessed are the celibates who masturbate
for they shall inherit their due pleasures
without incurring bodily taxes
without martyring themselves
to the twisted beliefs of the masses.

May their bodies writhe and shine,
mouths utter mantras of shameless beauty
may they wear no lover's ring
nor vow nor bow, but stand reverent,
fingers curled in a labour of love.

Tranquil Sea

How many marriages survive on sedatives?
He's holed-up in a shed digesting a hot breakfast
she's left cold on a shelf of cleaning fluids.

Her only trophy, the pride of the mantle-piece,
their long gone son in grey school uniform.

Midday, he is a moray eel thrusting his face
through the kitchen doorway.
I hope lunch is ready on time today?
She reddens like a cooked crab.

She tidies around his elbows, whips plates like pucks
onto the table as he shoots his requests.
Where? Where is the gravy, woman?

A rare monster, to be fed, groomed, milked.
She expected more. Marriage seemed a fine castle
from the outside but once inside, the walls interned her.
She needs more than magic to cool this dragon's breath.

A brown bottle, another winter's day.
Glass drips. Head lowered, she notices nothing,
her gloved hands buried in tepid dishwater.
She's dead calm, no change forecast.

Bridgewater Station

Walking three miles in the rain to say goodbye
and walking into the clouds like a sodden boot,
I celebrate our aqueous romance, always trudging
to reach a warm hearth, to peel off grey selves.

Never enough leather between the two of us
to make it to the border, and the courtesy bus
doesn't pick up bare footed hobos. We made it
to summer then fought to bring back the mud.

When you left there were swallows in the eaves
building a nest of wire and hair – our bed,
with my hook and bone and books of poems
and your heavy knapsack, always packed.

Do you feel in our numb departing skin
a steady beat, reliable as this train that rolls in
like a long striped stocking? *I'll write*
you a poem a day, you say. I kick my tongue,

kiss your rain-smacked lips and taste the city.
Already a chill sweet blain, in memory of you.
You'll never know that my great splashing strides
widened when I thought your train was coming.

Tree as Saviour

How many lives
are spared by the grace of trees?
People cling sweatily over raging bulls, rivers, rhinos;
or embrace a bonsai trunk on a sheer cliff face praying for strength
of arms and roots. Walls in the buttress trunk of the *Ficus* fold to hide
a fugitive. Hollow logs nurse lost children through black frost nights.
Huon pine masts sail the ship-wrecked to shore. Twigs feed
the flame at the feet of a frozen mountaineer.
And the twisted horse-chestnut
branches into ladders
for lovers who
climb to
leafy
heights
beyond
the realms
of earth-
bound
minds.

Travelling Back

for Sheryl

In pale morning light I drop my pack and lean
on an overgrown gate. I can almost see
a woman's face through long gone lace, broken glass
where a kitchen would once have glowed warm
and wafted out aromas of preserves and pickles.

Did she carry those two metal pails
to the creek, perfectly balanced
on the scales of her fore-arms?
I take a drink from the yellowish pool
taste iron from the tumbled tool-shed.

Ethereal fingers of sun touch stone walls
and the grave of this old shack sighs.
I see them now, at the mossy railing fence
his arm around her mended cardigan,
sweat-ringed hats tilted towards a vegie patch.

Further along the track, I pass through
their sallow orchard, an archive of moss
and lichen shrouded in bridal creeper.
My invasion is felt in the boggy depths.
I carry their seeds onward, inside and out.

Oyster Bay

for Daniel

From the shack across the bay
it takes two hours to walk the gritty spit.
On a moon spiced night, I tread pearl sand
watch the fan of lights on water
a town afloat in black.

I hear a mopoke in *Callitris* pines
like a faint fog horn
through waves pounding the rocks.
I find the Southern Cross
and the Big Dipper,
taste the salt marinated air.

The moon weakens behind cloud
until I can barely see my way
only the mopoke's call
clear as a lighthouse
leads me back to my tin shack
where you wait
on the bottom bunk.

Feet

like to meet
other feet under
blankets or long table-
cloths they are not
possessive like hands
do not shake with
everyone they meet
some demand lovers
to lick arches or nibble
on knobbly pink digits
many poor soles are
addicted to massage oils
and prostitute themselves
for a fondle in front of tv
but feet can be sharp
with their ten red talons
and must not be rubbed
the wrong way.

Nipples

for Honey G

Nipples are not on-off buttons
they are radio dials waiting to be tuned in.
Nipples are not raisins
they are glacé cherries on frosted cup cakes.
Nipples are not freckles
they are beauty spots on powdered cheeks.
Nipples are not rivets
they are marshmallows to roll on the tongue.
Nipples are not bulldogs
they are seal-point Siamese, soft and strokeable.
Nipples are not beans
they are chocolate stars, caramel buds, aniseed rings.
Nipples are not pebbles
they are lustrous pearls glistening in the shower.
Nipples are not shy
they are brave sherpas leading women on journeys.

The Head Mistress's Speech
circa 1975

As the school social approaches
it is timely to remind you girls:

No minis, no denim, no platforms.
No gaudy eye make-up nor spidery lashes.
No see-through fabrics. No strapless dresses.
We are not living in Caligula's time.

No G strings. No briefs.
No patent leather shoes
or the boys will see the reflections
from under your dresses.

No liquor. No cigarettes.
And remember
no close dancing – an elbow's
length apart. I will be checking.

And don't let me see you hanging around
giggling all night in the Powder Room.
You must dance. I have taught you all the steps.

The Gods

Burnt out from the manufacturing industry,
pushing buttons, mixing dangerous chemicals
dodging asteroids and all for a low wage, the gods
threw down their tools and walked off the job.
They strove long enough to prove
they could produce varieties of anything
could keep the line operating night and day.

No wonder they shut themselves
in their celestial lounge-rooms. No more miracles.
Why should they? May as well vegetate
in front of a big blue screen, replaying endlessly
the images of their creations.
But they're lonely. No human wise enough
for a decent chat, and besides the gods know
everything before it's said.
And they can't get along together either.

So alone they stay,
staring at the soapies which they've produced
deleting scenes and cast on the whim of a yawn
changing stations on the suffering
and turning down the colour on the depressed.
Mostly, they have the sound off altogether.

B C*

My windows have web sites
with real, not virtual, spiders.
They will inject more than ink
into my scream if I try to delete
with bare fingers.
My lap top is a cat, her paws
the only pads a mouse encounters
in this house.

*Before Computer

Next to Godliness

Bowed in respect to the Scriptures
I drip sweat as the dragon roars.

Like footprints in the sand
futile patterns against the nap
crisscross and overlap.
I poke my all-consuming wand
at sinful crumbs
evil clumps of hair,
purging a pathway
to an inherited dream
of unblemished surfaces.
On my weekly pilgrimage
along the sunlit hallway
I curse dust, gravity,
the messy sheddings of nature,
kick the stool and slam the door.

A blockage and bag-change
bring me back to my knees.

Wing Spans

Most times, I'm a paltry garden fowl
endlessly pecking my quarter acre:
a beetle, a milk thistle, enough to strive for.

But alone on my perch, I dream of alter-eagles
circling the coop, traversing the roof
I am *Aquila audax*
casting a black crucifix on the hill below,
my eyes, claws and beak, scimitar sharp.
Part of the swirling atmosphere
I soar on endorphin currents.

I vow to stay up here where air is clear
but a rooster crows and chics peep
and my mystery flight is placed on standby.

I Want MORE

More eye to eye, mind to mind conversations
when the odd tear or missing pulse
drowns the air with passion.
More walks in summer forests,
along evening seashores,
more experiences of the soul.

I want to see my friends'
back teeth, their bellies shaking
with epidemic laughter.
I want to cry, snort, wet my pants,
sing, hum and scream;
find Paul Robeson in my feet
and Kate Bush in my hair.

I want more sex that begins in the eyes
then spreads to mouth and fingers,
a journey that takes my skin through
textured layers and teases
the fine hairs on my neck and toes.

I want to find the family tree
uproot it, study it,
roll a cigarette with a leaf
toast the aunt who bequeathed me
her long diamante cigarette holder.

I want more miracles
to get me through this tough adulthood,
more psychic moments
that lift me cloud high
to wing with a coven of crows.

Stations

Sometimes, I'm in the London Underground, bright lights, the squealing black dust brakes of a dozen engines all pushing for space in peak hour cranium nerve ends. The mind's illusion of perpetual motion. I'm fired up – each track a possible journey. A handful of tickets, can't choose one direction, I want to split my thoughts and explore. Other times it feels like I'm travelling home on the slow seaward track. So what if I board another train half way? I may take that back-waters line out past the harbour where prickly weeds grow tall amongst the hulls of childhood, past leaning tin fences and dingy back yards, not made-up tarts with full-frontal press button garages and manicured lawns. And again the train diverts from its course.

A poet, I've come to like the ring route, out from reality and back again. Clickity Clickity Click went the sleek, fast engine of my youth as I sped around sweeping corners without realising how close to the edge I was. Gaining steam, I hung out of windows breathed in lungfuls of cold air, creative lust. Free to jump off at any station. I roared through dark moaning tunnels, non-stop through the eye of a storm. Then that first coupling. We slowly chug chug chugged uphill, toward the ultimate peak, the thrill of the downhill. How quickly I learnt the physics of love and gravity. Up and down, up and down all those hills and dells. Another carriage, another driver. The optimism of youth keeping me stoked. Where will I go? I don't know.

Then the train derails, a bloody mess. The shock of birth, and I know I'll never return to the place where I boarded. The new journey is perilous, the track shaky, rattly. I'm lost and there's so many flimsy bridges to cross. No schedules run to time. Round and round on the turn-table I spin. Working hard, carrying my load, yet getting nowhere. Then mid-journey, just when I thought those old routes had closed forever, the train slows, the load lightens and I veer back to the deeply familiar. I see the lights of towns I've left behind. I drive the engine alone now, take long scenic diversions to nature, pages and self. The lines are shiny again. There's more time to think. I learn that speed does not mean wisdom.

When sleepers loosen and straw daisies grow, where once were actions or poems, I'll crawl snail-slow along wet rails. I'll taste each leaf, speak with the ghosts of those whose luminous trails crossed my own. I might lose track of time but this train will have no number up front, no emergency stop. It will weave through night forests full of eyes and past the sunny slums of memory. Then finally, back to the first small siding where my mother waits in an apron with my case. Few will remember my busy schedule but I'd like to think that a little of my cargo will remain: a piece of coal to warm someone's feet or a dog-eared book by a bedside lamp.

Faces of a Church

On spring Saturdays, Mendelssohn plays
and two figures stand, sunbathed in blessings
ankle deep in dandelions and confetti.

At Christmas, windows mirror candle flame
and the congregation seems to float
above polished pews their voices cradled
high in wooden arches. Cherub children,
eyes lowered, glow with sinless fluorescence.

Today, headlights blaze through midday
a heat haze on the white gravel path
as another is placed in the marble garden.
A single cloud is speared by the dark bell tower,
a lone crow roosts on the wrought iron ridge.

Diary of a Maid

Asia Minor

Today, the sun was kind, yesterday's cloud severed by its radiance. Again I sewed for Judith, widow of Bethulia, working my threads from the first blush of dawn to crepuscular vespers. The bodice is finished and hangs on a hook behind the door, the neckline dives deeper than any I have sewn before. As I fitted the lining of her skirt, a blackbird sang from a high bough and I blessed each stitch on these cumquat layers where already a sheath is concealed like a snake in autumn leaves . . . Tonight, I heard the widow, speaking to the spirits: 'Dear husband, give me strength,' she pleads. And when she visits me, she removes her widow's weeds, tries the dress at every stage, parades before me in faces humble, brave and terrified.

☾ ☾ ☾

Tomorrow I will line the palm-rope basket strong enough to hold bread, wine, roasted grain, a cornucopia of roots and fruits, every last we have. I'm certain the basket will carry her quarry . . . I saw him once through a spy-hole in the wall which protects and pens us like animals for the slaughter. He smiled, and hailed Nebuchadnezzar as they nailed the shepherd's limp son to a high post. I will pad the basket with powdered orris root to absorb any juices that may spill.

☾ ☾ ☾

A New Moon last night blessed our return. At sunrise, the Assyrian army fled when they found Holofernes, felled like a giant palm tree, a ring of red around his headless trunk. Judith's smile of triumph set the bells singing. And she told me that his astonished face changed from lust to fright, as it rolled.

☾ ☾ ☾

The Sabbath. After thirty-four days, a stream of dusty people poured through the gates to celebrate freedom gained and fields reclaimed. They drank like beasts from the springs. And deep into the green well Judith threw the fiery dress. Our work put to rest in quiet water. And Holoferne's skull lies inside my woven nest, in a rocky crevice ninety-two cubits west of Bethulia . . . Tomorrow I will begin a night-gown of gossamer blue for our saviour Judith of Judah, so she may rise to the stars and sleep soundly again on the feathery down of the milky way.

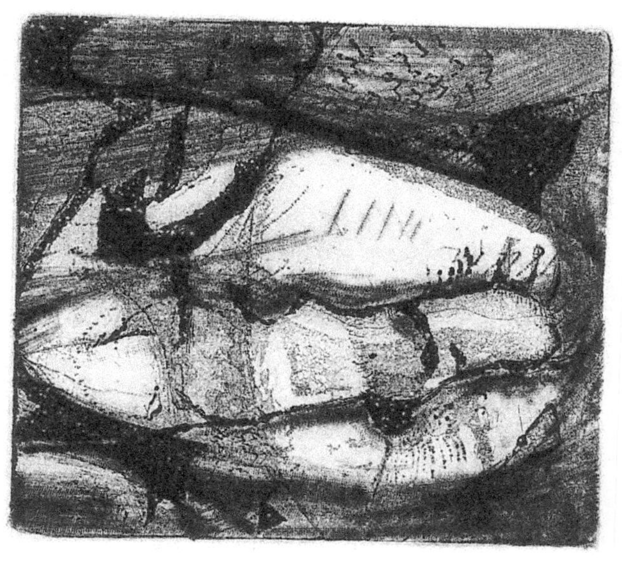

Seeds

Olive

Olea europaea

Black shrouded women kneel at her feet
praise and glean the wisdom of her age.
She nods to the other gnarled ones,

> *See how they still come to us*
> *we who fought through time*
> *to spare their hungry fathers.*
> *We drive away lightening for them.*
> *We know the moods of mother earth*
> *the slow blue flicker*
> *of her Mediterranean blood.*

On this burnished limestone slope
she gathers memories from centuries
of exposed living, of hard-won survival.
She works the stones without the luxury of a soft bed;
oils the long black hair of village girls;
and in drought years, clings to grim hope.
Yet each autumn she sings under the beat of wings
gives away fistfuls of hard-earned currency.

> *I made the long pilgrimage*
> *to this mountain small and barren.*
> *In the claws of a raven*
> *I came*
> *and grew for you.*

Garlic

Allium sativum

I am high priest of the creed *Amaryllis*
ordained through time and myth
to watch at your window, guard your neck,
hang around the cradles of sick babies.
Inside my thin robes I carry a white pouch
of angels' tears – a mystical heart, each segment
blessed and sure to cure plague, ward off death.

My skin is flaky and dry but inside I shine.
Plant me in your psyche. I'm the hero who saved
your ancestors from witches; was under
the sheets at your grandmother's birth.
I spring from the spot where Satan's left foot falls
and I will never be crushed. I will preach on roadsides
under bridges, even chopped up or tried by fire
my name remains on the lips of my persecutors.

Guarding the Corn Dollies

Zea mays

Man size stalks rasp as I pass.
They are guarding their daughters.
Listen, they whisper
as wind ruffles dry leaves:
There are crows in the air.
Stay swaddled my girls
in your raffia skirts.
Stay hidden under the veils
of your silky blonde hair.
Soon your beauty will shine
so bright, every gold hunter
will come to consume you.

Under autumn sun the ripening girls call
to their lovers. They have already begun
the dance of shedding layers.

A sweet pagan goddess
with long yellow plaits
awaits the first hungry mouth.

Cauliflowers

Brassica oleracea

In white caps and green cravats
haughty necked intellectuals

rise high in rows above dirt
climb ladders of stalk skyward.

The progeny of brain storms:
huge skulls, ridged, lumpy.

A phrenologist's dream.
A surgeon's first cut.

Perfect heads blade-severed
by the hundred, brisk to market

sold quickly, before worms
turn pure matter putrid and grey.

Pumpkins

Cucurbita

1.
Like bags of stolen gold
the butternuts hide on the hillside.
Come nightfall, they like to stroll
heave their heavy bottoms
past sluggish cabbages
in search of cinderella
or at least a silver leaf
filled with dew drops
in which to see
their own curvaceous reflections.

2.
Queensland blue,
a triple posterior with cold
muscular folds, formed
from the pure magic
of a frail yellow flower
which trumpets a tiny swelling
and within two moons
this babe weighs a stone
thinks it owns the vegie patch
expects to be hallowed.

The Murphy Brothers

Solanum tuberosum

Reliable underground workers
miners of poor man's gold
good breeders, tough skinned
dust hardy, can handle bruises
black eyes, incarceration
over long dark winters
huddled together under hessian;
will not crack under pressure
survive, dry humoured
well rounded – but will shoot
if given a chink to freedom.
Heads together, these lads
are always plotting to rise up
and take over the world.

Beetroot

Beta vulgaris

A gift for Grecian Gods,
this plumb-bob root
was famed for purging evils
from livers and spleens.

Now the bright blood bubble
comes sliced in a can.
It bleeds through burgers
in showy displays of martyrdom
cries for the beef patty
spreads pink guilt onto the bacon.

Without this bulb, borscht would pale
and sandwich trays seem grey.
Barbecues would be too dry,
bread wouldn't blush or mush.

Despite being the butt
of crude jokes and fake blood tricks
this cerise root is art on a plate.

Pomegranate

Punica granatum

A cache of jewels
packed tight in a leather pouch.
An old prospector's purse
full of hoarded garnets.

But no modern market
can be bothered
no teller has time
to weigh up the small change
of taste without returns.

Nowadays everyone wants
big, fleshy, seedless
eat on the run –
Who has time to sup slowly
to savour the unusual
the minute, the subtle
the pink gelled seed
of this strange apple?

Grapefruit

Citrus paradisi

Catapulted from tree tops
these bitter bombs can concuss
and worse if you try to eat them.
Loaded with calorie-killing
taste-bud annihilating acid,
these face-crumpling grenades
should be detonated with caution.
Beware the tracer of juice
aimed to blind a man at two paces.

Anyone who can swallow
these medicine balls
shall win the battle, be bulgeless
and reflect the benefits
of supreme sacrifice, of offering
their tongue for this sharp fruit
to take out its frustration
at being green with envy
at its enemy: the sugary,
ostentatious orange.

Bananas

Musa sapientum

Bananas
hang like handfuls
of yellow rubber gloves
blown up and stuck to a home-made tree
with torn crepe paper leaves –
a cardboard prop in a kindy play.

Bananas like to clown about
think they own the cartoon market.
Some bananas do erotic dances
yet they often slip up, become pedantic
about where they'll perform
or who they'll strip for.

Beach babes at heart
they insist on sunshine
and thrive on Hollywood romance
get depressed at the first cold snap
and turn dark, mushie, ooze misery
through their thin aging skins.

Figs

Ficus carica

the large soft leaves of the fig tree
were velveteen underwear
for Adam and Eve

the naked fruit wears no shame
its veins are strong, pulsing with seed
a thousand purple pouches
hang for your delight

these fruits are pregnant questions
waiting for the inquiries
of beaks and fingers

they are fed through
a green hose of stem
and swell from a sugar drip
until they drop, plop
on their soft bottoms

but deep down the fig family
can be clingy, possessive
with too much vigour
for their own good
some have even been known
to strangle their closest friends.

Melon

Cucumis

moon
melon   seed mother
moist   ripe small split hole
to sweetness curl tongue   sup slowly
flesh juicy   liquid velvet   finger slippery
lip luscious   palpable penetrable   lick inside
underside   wet skin   squeeze   lush   plush
chin drip   ripple soft   melting melon   open

Ginger

Zingiber officinale

Sister of Mandrake
curvaceous, ambidextrous
a Shiva dancer, multiple armed
poised to snap into rhythm.
Her perfume is pure pheromone.
Zesty is her middle name.
She's a singer, a zinger
she stirs, she fries.
Through endless nights
she flavours the stages
of cheap Asian cafes.
She's been seen
dancing with Fred Astaire.
She mixes with a hot crowd.
She can be eaten whole.

Prickly Pear

Opuntia inermis

Studded jacket, five o'clock shadow
nerve tip anger outward bristling:
So what if I'm small, I've enough seed
to plant a desert – to sow every field.
I'm Fabio, Casanova, rolled into one.
Stay away you Cactoblastis puritans.
I'm a cowboy's testicle on a cartoon cactus.
Don't mess with me – I shoot fruit bandits.
I won't give up to gloved hands, long tongs;
even drawn and quartered, I leave my mark.

Outside the Market, 7 am

Don't worry luv
their ears go blue
when they're dead,
the market man says
as I gape down
at a rag wrapped
old man, sprawled
on frosty grass.

See, red as chilli peppers.
Just pickled, luv.
He kicks
an empty bottle
and winks
then crosses the busy street
pushing a barrow
of fresh dewy fruit.

Creature acts

Fish Tank

I feed two goldfish
flakes of corn and ice-cream wafer.
The snail, alone for years
has just given birth – a hundred
crawling pebbles emerged
to do their spot of window wiping.
At night the fish glide
to the piano side, Chopin choreographs;
as they gulp in time,
twirl through hollow Nullarbor rock.
A poster of glittering fairies
is blue-tacked behind the glass.
Is my world any less absurd than theirs?

Release at Cudlee Creek

After the last harvest of walnuts in the autumn grove
white clouds of cockatoos and corellas drift north;
the sly tide of rats laps at the nutting shed door.
Cold nights, hungry grey skies. Wild birds are braver.

A shabby sulphur-crested cockatoo stays in the valley –
balding and grubby, it crash lands in a heap
of autumn leaves to scrape and scratch
amongst husks and black nuts.
Perhaps a cache lies hidden beside a log.
Then the bird works its malformed beak
with nut held tight between toes, makes a hole
no bigger than a one cent piece, hooks out golden flesh.

When May winds undress the grove, when every wet leaf
is overturned, every nut drilled, the old cockatoo
night-roosts on a low red-gum stump, its breastbone
a line of symmetry for the fox to divide.

Beginnings and Endings?

A light bulb with intricate filament
was the first sun she worshipped
when her mouth and fingers
knew more than ears and eyes.
When the curtains were open
she'd marvel at jigsaw puzzles of leaves
butterflies like jumbo jets
and colours beyond the realms of crayons.

At Christmas, she'd step inside glass baubles
to a world of glitter-snow
lifetimes away from a hot kitchen
where blowflies darkened windows.
She kept two bright scarab beetles
(the only natural December sparkle)
in a blue cellophane-lined box
and in the dim light, thought she saw
Jesus kissing Cinderella.

Now, she holds the shirred hand
of her grandmother, feels
the ridged patterns as she leads
her down the hallway.
A gasp and creased smile tell her
that grandma still sees
the laden Christmas tree
through the bright fairy-light eyes
of a girl of five. *And so do I.*

Home Invasion

In the Bay of Biscay clay of the Adelaide plains
hidden under a layer of *Pittosporum* leaves
are scores of trap-doors, round as ten cent pieces.
Open the hinged lid with a twig, see silken padding
on underside, plush as a lined jewellery box.

As children, we'd coax with seeded grass
until we spied the oily black prosoma
of a *Mygalomorph*, hunched to jump.
I'd run swiftly, trembling.
Once, one sprung and clung to the hem
of my petticoat, rode my mad Tarantella
to the back door where I stripped and flicked.
Involuntary shudders followed for hours.

Next Guy Fawkes, my brothers avenged
studded the yard with three-penny-bungers
spiders ascending, smoking, staggering
like shell-shocked soldiers.
A harsh sentence for home defence.

King Gussie

The old tom cat's tail appeared at the window,
like a paintbrush gone stiff in jellied turps.
Gussie, returned from his crusade
mud dyed, howling, demanding a feast
as if a week's foray were a year on the battlefield.
Tipless tail, kinked midway; perforated ears
and a broad nose chequered with scars:
King Gussie, though often called lesser names
sprayed supreme, left his scent
and flew his bent flag on foreign blocks.

I think we witnessed his coronation,
one drizzly July day: a circle of twenty or so cats
crowded our backyard, growled and meowed
to their tabby king who crouched sphinx-still
in the middle, yowling deep and mournful
until one by one they slunk back over fences

In these days of the kitty litter tray and cat cage
I am proud of our old reprobate's innate ways
am privileged to have seen through flyscreen doors
Felis domesticus engaged in old lores.

Lullabies

for Max Fatchen

Like a ticking clock to an orphaned cat
the sound of rain on a tin roof
takes me back to my first bedroom
a corrugated-iron lean-to
where wind thrummed through louvres
and the moon was a comfort
peeping from a doorway of clouds.

My body curled around a hot water bottle
I perfected the game of shadows
saw wings as wide as eagles'
sweep past curtains;
under the street-light's yellow fog
were castles and beastly faces
sneering from the bare street tree.

A shy child, frightened of the dark,
these rhythms kept me safe
the breath beats of a clock,
the womb whoosh of raindrops.
Even now, I lie awake to listen,
in this era of tiled roofs, digital time
and pine for those old lullabies.

Alternative Barometers

for Bruce

Ants braille cement
crazy messages of tidal waves
and killer rain drops.

Women read the clouds
as they whirl wire hoists
gilled with clothes.

A kookaburra gargles
before midday
a waterfall of laughter
spills prophecies of rain.

When the moon's nipple
has a hazy pink aureola
the famished throats of creeks
will soon flow milky-brown.

Gum trees glow like gas-flame.
Grandfather's bones ache.
Cockies wheel and screech.
Seagulls flee the beach.

Cattle brace their backsides
as wind gusts anti-clockwise
and the whipping ringmaster
prods their hides. Clouds clap
from a spangled sky.

Seafaring Blood

A cold Sunday evening,
I watch two trawlers rise and fall at the jetty's end.
I float within, feel their rhythms under my skin.
I've ridden prawn trawlers, ferries, ocean liners
wind and sea-spray stiffening my hair.
These days, I am a shell washed to the hills
but I can still hear the sea inside.

I daydream back to the family trawler, *Karina*,
as the haul spills over deck: gloved hands sort,
fish flip like silver coins and blue pincers nip.
A chorus of gulls swoops and shrills above.
Then Uncle stoops by a crusted rudder,
scales on his sleeves. We leave a frothy wake
as he guides us past secret markers to shore.

A gull shrieks me back to this beach.
An hour has swept by, quick as sea-weed on the wind.
Suddenly I am cold, damp and late
because my sea-faring blood made me drive so far
out of my way to snort rank sea-weed, to absorb
the calming beat, pulse of an old friend.

Wooden Spoons

Worn thin on one edge and half green
the long thick spoon with finger grooves
stirred the steaming copper
dyed sheets, speared singlets.

Indoors, another spoon served soup
and measured occasional spankings.
This spoon was hidden in 68,
never returned nor mentioned again.

In cluttered drawers, my wooden spoons
are puny, disposable, superseded
by plastic ladles and modern theories
about corporal punishment.

Sunday Roast

His waist line was under his armpits
Great grey trousers billowed
beneath this false equator.
A leather belt held its ground
around 30 degrees north of his navel.

His orders were gospel.
Wedged between table and sideboard
he was known to slip that leather snake
from its looped track
and hang it slackly on the chair.

A warning in case his daughters broke
a glass, or spilt the soup.
His corned-beef cheeks aglow
he'd begin with verbal welts and progress
according to how much was left on his plate.

Sally would stop fidgeting with her sprouts.
Giggling Bonney would lower her eyes.
With each audible swallow the snake grew
the venomous buckle ready to strike.
May I leave the table, we'd plead one by one.

A–Z of Memorable Scents

A
Aunt Alison had that soap and talcum scent
of Coty fragrances from long ago, a dab of
rose-water on each wrist, a hint of camphor
on her cardigan collar as you kissed her goodbye.

B
Books, yellowed and musty or new and inky
I let my nostrils roam and dance along shelves.
For forty years I've flipped cold pages close to my face
breathed in the print and dusty rooms before me.

C
Chlorine brings back that blue round of plastic and water
which crouched on our back lawn. The adolescent swirl
of open-mouthed laughter. Hot nights, cheap sweet alcohol,
a rush of adrenalin at a brush of bare skin under ripples.

D
Dirt, good old sod, rich, black and wormy. Fingers in,
boots sinking deep in spring beds, a suctioning squelch
as you raise a leg. Or that damp mushroomy whiff as
you pitch-fork layers of luscious compost, steaming.

E
Eggs: curried, coddled, scrambled or poached.
Acrid and farty, the stronger the better.
Boiled green, or runny, sunny side up. Sulphuric,
bucolic, or old and reeking, splattered on a fence.

F
Feathers: my cheek on the pulsating purple-green
chest of a favourite pigeon, I breathe, heat my nose,
her breast; savour the musky scent and quick beat
inside this soft cave. I collect feathers, so I am rich.

G
Freshly mown grass. *Hashish* in Maltese.
Visitors eyes widened when nanna claimed her son
was out cutting the hashish. I'd pile the sweet clippings
into a bed, green views tinting my dreams ever since.

H
The hair of a loved one, the warmth within
as your own breath mingles with the human scent
so distinct to each head. From the talcum fuzz of a baby
to the sweet yellowed scalp of a winter grandmother.

I
Ironing: revaporising after-shave, or body odours in armpits.
The singed linen and curry aromas from neatly creased napkins.
A burst of steam and ti-tree oil and it seems this warm haze,
these rhythmic strokes were made for winters' afternoons.

J
The juices of love: salted capers, caviar and lemon zest.
The nose recalls innate pheromones; lost and ancient
recipes for temple perfumes. Breathe it. Live it.
Yet forget the spell when the trance ends.

K
Kerosene heater: that cage around a blue and purple
vapour haze which flickered like a skittish jelly-fish.
The dull headache from the closed-window warmth
as father feeds the Dalek with pink lolly water.

L
Lemon Myrtle. Citrus flavours are sprinkled world-wide
from the pithy Buddha's hand lime in the Himalayas
to our lofty sweet verbena tree *Backhousia citriodora*
with the zing and tang of a dozen lemons in every leaf.

M
Moss, my soul's food, I'll bury my nose, my fingers, my toes.
I'll quaff it and snort it, on the rocks or with trickling water
and fungi on great decaying black logs. This is my lung
alive to the pulse of primeval green.

N
Nicotine on the breath of my first boyfriend –
addicted before my first draw! I'd snort his smoky
jumper and kiss his Marlborough lips. Twenty years
of cigarettes, now abstinence; the death kiss finally over.

O
Onions: white fire, invisible sparks stinging
hurtling up through nostrils and into smarting eyes.
Fried, they bring my husband from afar, stir his juices.
Misty eyed, I am goddess of the stove awaiting kisses.

P
Pine needles, spruce cones, snapped green and inhaled
on a spongy brown mattress as I watch clouds amble by.
In the city, menthol cigarettes and Pine-o-clean:
the forest mimicked and filtered into mechanical chaos.

Q
Quince: nose to fuzz, I rub its jaundiced cheek
to my own, glean the cold, the hint of tart.
Old quinces smell like wine cellars, yet stewed
they are pure, sweet *bella rouge* blushing at the cream.

R
Rotten sandshoes from a teenage sockless wonder,
at the end of summer. Where is the dead animal?
Removed from feet, these damp puff balls explode
with stink-spores, clear the room, free the tv for him.

S
Swamp: rich, ripe and slightly septic. At Fisherman's Bay,
a rickety long-drop toilet perches near a mangrove tree.
At low tide the aroma is breathtaking, salty, over-marinated,
yet somehow sensual, earthy and essentially human.

T
Train Stations and country sidings, the cold diesel draught
whipping from tracks up skirts. Airborne black dust as wheels
squeal and you bridge the smoky gap with your heart in your
throat and walk to your seat triumphant at stopping the beast.

U
Urine, tom cat, in the car, in the sun, on the seat cover
you're sitting on. Or the faint urea breeze from father's nightly
verandah pees, on a summer evening with hot cement and
big spots of rain mixed with hints of eucalypt and lawn clippings.

V
Vacuuming in summer with a Cash Converters Hoover,
that dry tomb dust taste, sweat on my forehead.
A hot electrical scent, the rank whiff
as a mummified mouse is sucked from behind the fridge.

W

Wood smoke, in a cold kitchen. Any range's morning ash
gives off that waft of hickory and roasted nuts.
I shut my eyes and breathe in a thousand years:
this ghost of communion and cooking fires.

X

X-ray rooms smell of methylated spirits and antiseptic.
Left cold on the slab you can't help but wonder
about the lead apron, the little grey window
as you're numbed by the chemical clean, rays unseen.

Y

Yabbies come slime strung, reeking of greenish mud.
They are the plugs in the sump, dug deep in years
of detritus. Soft plopping bubbles give them away.
Netted, they rise, boxing with their can-opener fists.

Z

We camped behind a zoo one February night, heard
the big cats, sensed their pacings under full moon.
Through canvas walls, sad messages of damp straw
and warm dung arrived on a gentle zephyr.

Emu

He is expert at imitating the grass tree,
Xanthorrhoea stalk neck stretched high
a periscope to unexplored skies.
His space is truly lateral
his flight all runway.

Shaking a soft frilled skirt
over slender legs, a mismatch of elegance
and buffoon, he pirouettes for bread
flutters movie star lashes for the cameras.

Beneath two scaly grey stilts,
prehistoric feet branch out –
three leathery toes
flower-print the sand.

Deep round eyes are pools
of mistrust, the desert mirrored in one,
cyclone wire squares in the other.
His beak a sharpened mussel shell
ready to snap shut on the teasing child.

Poor *Yankirri*, who dances and sings for you now?
Who watches and tells of your every move?

Button Collection

for my mother

The tartan plaid biscuit tin rattles like rain as I walk.
A cloth is spread on the double bed and buttons hail,
strange little pebbles to be sifted and slowly sorted.
After a while our eyes magnify and we're in tiny town
where marcasite greys sparkle silver, and I must rub
the brown pretzels of leather jacket buttons,
hold mother of pearl to light and see rainbow ripples.
Rivalry between my children over who'll find the button
mum likes best and sheer elation if I sew it to a garment.

Sometimes I go back through a hole to my childhood
these inherited buttons hold a chestful of memories:
when my mother and I sat and plunged our fingers in.
Occasionally the bite of a hidden needle and I'd wait
for the red bubble. Two holes; four holes; all the little extras:
a crystal bead, a miniature cowry shell, bra hooks.
That soldier's button with the dented emblem –
Was he saved by this tiny shield? Two holes? Four holes?
My mother lived through *The Depression*, kept every zip,
strap, eyelet: unusable, but safe in this poet's hands.
So again I marvel at these dress-maker's jewels
and fasten a few more memories onto my own children.

Horologist

The ticks, tocks, whirrs and gongs
from fifty-odd clocks resounded
in my childhood home. Midnight began
at ten to twelve and ended at ten past.
The verbally abused cuckoo
returned defiantly every half hour
until its pine-cone pendulum
reached the lino and no-one but father
could pull the chain for *the wee birdie*.

He set his watch to the 5CL news,
performed the Sunday morning service
with a dust rag draped on his arm;
preached the virtues of each
and altered any wayward hands.
After a pre-ordained number of turns
he'd replace ornate keys to allotted vases.

In the oily aroma of his workroom
he monitored heartbeats
transplanted vital parts.
His invalid pension funded
springs, pins and brass escapements.
Blank white faces rested on shelves
waiting for the stroke of hands.

For decades, he sat at a felt covered bench
poring over tins of sorted springs,
cogs like serrated coins, one eye shut
the other adhered to a magnified lens.
Then suddenly his heart beat stopped
and one by one the clocks followed.

Locks and Keys

My father collected keys: from the silver hair pin
for an architect's pencil case, to the great bolt
that turned the crank on the stationary engine.
He loved the ornate loops and scrolls
on the brass keys from his antique clocks
held them up like shining pendants from other planets.
He worked in a car yard, couldn't bare to bin the spares
kept them jangling on hoops like some medieval jailer
always afraid the police would raid, suspect him a car thief,
his three skeleton keys smiling as they led him away.

As a child, this collection opened my imagination,
as I did the circuit of each jangling bracelet.
I'd pick favourites then begin to release birds
and beasts from cages, free starving convicts
and save my handsome prince from a witch's oven.
Later, our front door key, more fitted to a castle
than our cracked stucco, weighted down my handbag.
A good key has strength and weight, he'd say,
and how he hated Mr Minit and his cheap flat alloys.
He bent them with his big thumbs to prove their puniness.

The key to happiness however, was not in his collection,
caught in depression's turnstile, all doorways
closed except for those that led darkly inwards.
Suicide, his one successful jail-break.

The Mirning*

for Iris Burgoyne

Law, a hot, heavy overhead force strikes unexpectedly
like a meteor, to those who don't track the loose rules
of the system. Fences, what use, if a good stone cairn
can mark as well? And kangaroos don't rip their chests
nor black man wonder which side to stand.
Whales do not break laws, whatever the ocean offers
is free for all.

Mid 1800s, vast drifts of sand with senseless fences,
wallabies gone, hot sheep graze dry ground.
And four of these sunken-ribbed sheep go astray.
A frenzy of white tempered righteousness
blazes through mulga on horseback.
The posse raid the Mirning camp, demand to know,
'Who hunted today?'
Two hunters named. Two hunters hanged.
Not a mutton bone's worth of evidence.
When elders learn that their young men
are swinging in the town's main street, they ask,
Who is this bloke called Law?
told he's a judge from Adelaide sent to set an example.
That night, they creep into the judge's garden,
coax him out with animal calls and put a rope of *Law*
around *his* neck to settle the score.
Then return to camp to console the wailing mourners.

Gun shots wake sleeping families, horses gallop
through bark humpies. Flames. Screaming.
Men, women and children running naked and dazed
as they are driven to the cliffs of Elliston.

Massacres are usually so red but not this one
their dark bodies sweep the clear blue sea
as the tide takes them way out to where the whales swim
and sing with no mission, no roads
just ancient blood tracks winding below skin
calling them to roam free.

A few years later a white man
admits to his mates that he thieved the sheep
– was hard up trying to start a flock.

*the tribal name of the Aboriginal people of SA's west coast. Their totem is the whale. This story has been retold many times, although there is no documented evidence of the massacre.

Where do they go?

for Joan

Where do they go, those in comas
limp lipped, bloated from drips and drugs?
Are they making dandelion chains
in some childhood afternoon
chasing Shep the kelpie
while Mother spreads a picnic cloth?
Or are they high up in the corner
of their white walled room?
Do they see our forced smiles
hear quavering colloquialisms
as we try every trick of willpower
for just a flicker of eyelids?

The distance between us
like a lunar ocean.

Where do they go, those in comas,
wired like Gulliver to a tilted bed?
Do they rattle the windows of semi-death,
begging to step into familiar scenes?
Or beat and scratch to be free
from the ribs of a cage that binds them?

The respirator gasps,
I kiss your hollow hand.
Goodbye.

Evensong

I stitch an invisible seam as I tap my eucalypt stick
along this autumn street. Early evening is embroidered
with wood-smoke ribbons, the tiny bells of crickets.

Aged grass glows biblical yellow as a heat-wave sweeps
under a cool thatch of new cloud. An opaline sky jaggers
with light, a choir of crows hark hark a rebirth.

I am a tall shadow in the low-slung light of late afternoon.
The under-sides of petals glow. The chenille sky
is edged with tassels of carmine cloud.

Human transparencies shine from curtained frames.
A television smudges the still life in that hour
of communion before blinds are drawn.

I glance in, a voyeur of moments, patterns,
in each patch of this quilt of yards. The moon
is the tip of an egg in a nest of chimneys.

Between gate posts, a white orb weaver sets her round table.
And I wish for more evenings like this, to drift ghostly
on this humble and homely stage,

to play the role of no-one, but shine inside
at the thought of my part, my walk so brief
with a storm sniffing at my heels.

Author's note

Sincere thanks to everyone who has directly or indirectly helped in the creation of these poems or the production of this book.

As a recipient of an Australian Society of Authors mentorship grant in 2002, I was fortunate to work with WA poet Andrew Taylor. I thank Andrew for his excellent editorial advice and for his graciousness. I am grateful to the ASA for providing the mentorship program.

Thank you to the SA Writers' Centre and Friendly Street Poets for their tireless support and for providing the opportunities to meet and enjoy other writers; and to the members of First Draft for their valuable criticisms and encouragement.

My thanks and admiration to Franz Kempf, Adelaide artist, for the superb etchings. Also to Jan Owen, Roger Zubrinich, and to Michael, Stephanie and the staff at Wakefield Press for their ongoing support.

Special thanks to author Iris Burgoyne whose book *The Mirning* inspired my poem by the same title.

I thank my family for giving me inspiration and for putting things into perspective: my husband Daniel for his support and musical accompaniments over the years; my children Jasmine and Giles for letting me retreat to my study to write (sometimes); Ken, Ray and Bruce for their proofreading skills; and my dear friends, Sheryl, Junice and Yasmin for being there. I thank my cat Piecroft for keeping my lap warm.

Jude Aquilina, 2004

Acknowledgements

Poems in this collection have been published in the following newspapers, journals and anthologies: *Art State*, *Blue Dog*, *The Canberra Times*, *Centoria*, *Elders Stock Journal*, *Famous Reporter*, *Friendly Street Anthologies 24–28*, *The Herald*, *Illness A Journal*, *The Leader*, *Muse Magazine*, *Panorama*, *Poetrix*, *Redoubt*, *Social Alternatives*, *Spinning Thistledown*, *Tamba*, *Tears in the Fence* (UK), *The Colonial Athens*, *The Mount Barker Courier*, *The Shimmering*, *Vernacular*, *Wildfire* and have been broadcast on Radio Adelaide, Three D, Triple B and Radio RPH.

Wakefield Press is an independent publishing and
distribution company based in Adelaide, South Australia.
We love good stories and publish beautiful books.
To see our full range of books, please visit our website at
www.wakefieldpress.com.au
where all titles are available for purchase.
To keep up with our latest releases, news and events,
subscribe to our monthly newsletter.

Find us!

Facebook: www.facebook.com/wakefield.press
Twitter: www.twitter.com/wakefieldpress
Instagram: www.instagram.com/wakefieldpress

www.ingramcontent.com/pod-product-compliance
Ingram Content Group Australia Pty Ltd
76 Discovery Rd, Dandenong South VIC 3175, AU
AUHW020208230226
423697AU00001B/8

9 781862 546400